The Beautiful
California
Missions

CONTENTS

BEAUTIFUL AMERICA PUBLISHING COMPANY

CURRENT BOOKS

Utah, Oregon, Alaska, Hawaii, Arizona, Montana, Michigan, Colorado, Washington, California, No. California, San Francisco, British Columbia, California Missions, Western Impressions, Lewis & Clark Country

FORTHCOMING BOOKS

Vancouver, B.C., Massachusetts, So. California, Pennsylvania, Minnesota, Wisconsin, Maryland, Kentucky, Georgia, Florida, Illinois, Texas, Ohio

Send for Complete Catalog 50c

Beautiful America Publishing Company
202 N.W. 21st Avenue, Portland, Oregon 97209

The Beautiful
California
Missions

Text by Lee Foster

Published by Beautiful America Publishing Company
202 N.W. 21st Avenue, Portland, Oregon 97209
Robert D. Shangle, Publisher

Second Printing

ISBN 0-915796-22-8 (paperback)
ISBN 0-915796-23-6 (hard bound)
Library of Congress Catalog Card Number
78-102341

PHOTO CREDITS

INTRODUCTION

In the late 1760s it became apparent to the Spanish King, Charles III, that the unknown lands in Alta, or Upper, California might be settled either by the Russians, who were venturing farther south from the Bering Sea each year in their search for otter skins, or the English, who had recently won control of Canada.

To forestall the advance of these competing nations the king gave permission to the Franciscan Order to develop missions in California. He weighed the decision carefully because Spain was in the twilight century of its colonial adventure in New Spain, as the present Mexico was then called. All commitments and investments of Spain's dwindling resources and manpower had to be considered. The relatively modest cost of financing missions made that system attractive to the king.

A mission allowed Spain to control the land, asserting a right to ownership by fact of occupation, requiring only the manpower of two padres and a few protective soldiers. After some years of investment in supplies, the mission was to become self-sufficient. The priest was to educate and Christianize the natives, training them for ten years in agriculture and self-sufficiency. After this period the mission lands and improvements were to be turned over to the natives as a self-governing unit of Spanish subjects. The Franciscans, who wanted to save souls, and the king, who sought to secure the land, joined together in an alliance of mutual benefit.

Today a Californian, visitor to California, or reader of Californiana who wishes to comprehend both the bountiful heritage of the Golden State and the present life patterns of California people should take the time to acquaint himself with the 21 Franciscan missions founded between 1769 and 1823.

The first enduring outposts of European culture in the West, the missions are today only symbolic of the influential establishments they had become by 1832. All of the missions can be visited by interested travelers. Restoration efforts have proceeded with varying completeness, relatively thorough at La Purisima, for example, but merely started at Soledad.

The influence of the missions on California has been both obvious and subtle. The names and locations of the major California cities, from San Diego to San Francisco, were determined by mission sites. Parts of U. S. 101, the primary highway, follow El Camino Real, the original King's Road that joined mission sites, spaced about a vigorous day's walk apart.

Other mission influences are less readily apparent. A tradition of California hospitality began with the missions, where travelers in early-day California could find sustenance at no expense. The grain and vegetable agriculture so central to California's present economy developed first in the vast wheat, barley, corn, bean, and pea fields of the missions. The padres also demonstrated that cattle and sheep could be raised profitably for their hides and meat, breeding herds that reached the amazing number of 151,180 head of cattle and 137,969 sheep by 1832.

The mission-style architecture, emphasizing heavy walls, arcades, red roof tiles, and extensive overhangs to protect from sun and rain has been perpetuated in prominent California institutions, such as Stanford University, and in many private ranch-style houses throughout the state. And an acquaintance with men the stature of mission-founders Junipero Serra or Fermin Lasuen cannot help but influence the concepts with which we define our own lives.

CALIFORNIA MISSIONS

San Diego de Alcala *(first mission, 1769).*

Location: In Mission Valley, off Interstate 8.

Two overland parties and three ships set out from south Baja to convene at San Diego Bay in July 1769, but the adventure of establishing a new mission territory was blunted by the harsh price these pioneers paid. Of the three ships, two met with ill fortune. The *San Jose* was lost at sea with all her men and valuable supplies, and the *San Carlos* was blown off course, finally reaching her goal with her crew dead or dying of scurvy. Only the *San Antonio* arrived expeditiously to assume the role of caretaker for the beleaguered survivors. Of the 90 crewmen, 60 died of scurvy. The overland parties suffered the rigors of the Baja desert and sustained heavy losses.

Undaunted, those able-bodied enough to participate witnessed a simple ceremony whereby the land was claimed by the military governor, Gaspar Portola, for Spain. Shortly thereafter the father president of the missions, Junipero Serra, blessed a nearby site for the first mission. This division of authority between a secular and sacral leader proved troublesome throughout the mission period. When Serra for example, wanted to found a mission in the Santa Barbara region the governor decided that such a venture would overextend his small garrison of troops.

Five years after the first founding, the mission was moved six miles inland to a site better watered and farther from the unruly garrison of troops, who had an unfortunate influence on the new Indian converts, called "neophytes". Throughout mission history there was constant abrasive contact between Indians and some elements of the garrisons.

As the San Diego Mission attracted more and more neophytes, some Indians hostile to them burned the mission in November 1775 and crowned the brief career of padre Louis Jayme with martyrdom, making Jayme the first martyr of Spain's California mission program.

After a two-year retreat to the presidio, (the garrison fort of the soldiers), the priests ventured back to the charred site and, with the help of the once-hostile Indians, who saw by now that the Spanish muskets could not be overcome, rebuilt the mission and eventually established a branch mission, or *asistencia,* at Santa Ysabel some 60 miles east.

Today the traveler at the San Diego Mission is greeted by a spare but inviting white church, (recently declared a basilica), an impressive set of bells in an adjacent tower, attractive gardens, and a small museum of artifacts.

What caused the mission system to disintegrate? The immediate cause was the secularization law, which went into effect in 1834, destroying in a few years what 65 years of patient work had created. The plan of the missions, to turn the Indians into a self-governing, self-sufficient unit that would be ready to take ownership control of the land in 10 years, proved difficult of realization in California. Communications lines with Spain were slow and the supplies sent were penurious. Approval of mission plans by military governors was often delayed. Fire, drought, and earthquake set many of the individual missions back after years of progress. Diseases brought in by whites, such as measles and smallpox, killed many Indian neophytes. And the California Indian was temperamentally so removed from an organization mentality that the Indians could not in a short time learn to manage the complex mission affairs.

So the 10-year timetables passed, long overextended by 1834. Additionally, the vast holdings in grain and cattle that the missions accumulated were ripe plums to be picked by the numerous sons of prolific Spanish secular pioneers who came to California to live in the pueblos, small towns set up adjacent to each mission and presidio. Spain's power was waning, a liberal Mexico gained her independence, and the Act of Secularization became inevitable.

The reality of secularization fell far short of the intention, which was still to turn over at least a portion of the land and cattle to individual Indian families. A civil administrator appointed to oversee the transition at each mission could not, even if he wished, prevent the Indians from quickly selling their land and property to speculators. Franciscan fathers of Spanish origin were quietly expelled and the Indians were left without the disciplined guidance that had built the system. Herds and grains were quickly appropriated by local Spanish residents.

San Luis Rey de Francia (18th mission, 1798).

Location: 5 miles east of Oceanside on State Highway 76.

Though it is convenient to discuss the missions from south to north, starting with the first and most southerly mission, San Diego, and ending with the last and most northerly, San Francisco de Solano, it would be a mistake to assume that the missions developed from south to north in a geographical sequence.

After San Diego the scene shifted to Monterey Bay, then the northern frontier, with the founding of Mission San Carlos Borromeo de Carmelo, the Carmel Mission. The story would then continue at nearby San Antonio de Padua, then jump south to the Los Angeles area and Mission San Gabriel. To avoid this geographic jumping we are moving steadily south to north. San Luis Rey was the second mission in the south-to-north line, but the 18th to be founded. The year was 1798.

San Luis is called with justification the "king of the missions". The Spanish missionaries were painstaking bureaucrats who totaled annually the records of each mission. By 1832 San Luis Rey's data were impressive, showing more livestock than any other mission, fully 57,330 cattle, sheep, goats, pigs, horses, and mules. On the eve of secularization San Luis was the most populous mission, with 2,788 neophytes.

Today the grounds give a traveler a good sense of the impressive institution that this mission became. The handsome cruciform church, a Spanish, Moorish, and Mexican blend, with its pleasing bell tower, has been restored. As with many of the missions, the property was eventually deeded back to the Catholic Church by the United States after California became a state. Because San Luis became a Franciscan seminary, much careful attention was lavished on restoration.

While visiting the mission gardens, which include the first pepper tree brought to California, an informed observer can imagine the scene in 1832. Adjacent to the large church, which seats 1,000, was a compound 500 feet square, fully six acres enclosed by arcades used for domestic crafts, lodgings, and food preparation. Across from the church stands an elaborate stone terrace that once functioned as an outdoor laundry (fed by springs), with a sunken garden, extensive adjacent fruit orchards, and a charcoal filtered drinking water system. "In the still uncertain light of dawn," wrote traveler Duhaut-Cilly in 1827, "this edifice . . . had the aspect of a palace."

San Juan Capistrano (seventh mission, 1776).

Location: On Interstate Highway 5, in the center of the town of San Juan Capistrano.

The history of San Juan Capistrano, founded by Junipero Serra in November of 1776, is a romantic tale that reaffirms how fragile the best-wrought works of man can be.

By 1806 the energetic padres, assisted by a gifted stone mason from Culiacan, Mexico, named Isidor Aguilar, had fashioned a stone church whose design surpassed in sophistication and professionalism that of any other edifice in California. The 180-foot by 40-foot cruciform structure had vaulted ceilings and seven domes cut from sandstone quarried six miles from the site. Four bells were elevated in a 120-foot tower, topped with a gilded cock weathervane, visible 10 miles away.

For the next six years, until a wintry morning in 1812, the great church of San Juan Capistrano gathered its neophytes for morning mass and inspired superlatives from all visitors. On the fateful day, as two young boys gripped the belltower rope to announce the call to mass, a severe earthquake in a year of several major quakes shook the tower and church. Walls swayed and the entire structure collapsed. Forty Indian bodies were recovered from the rubble. The work of the mission continued, but it was unthinkable that resources could again be mustered to rebuild the church. Divine services were returned to the little original adobe church, now called "Father Serra's Chapel" inasmuch as it is the only building still standing at any mission in which the founding father is known to have actually officiated.

The unchanging annual return of the swallows to Capistrano on St. Joseph's day each spring has been interpreted by innumerable romantics as a symbol of seasonal continuity. Unless the birds have been delayed in their flight from Argentina by an unseasonal tropical storm, they return to build their mud nests at San Juan with a dependability that allows major television and press scheduling of a media event for March 19.

One of the earliest reporters of life at San Juan Capistrano was New Englander Richard Henry Dana in his *Two Years Before the Mast.* Dana described the method by which dried cattle hides were transported down from the cliffs a few miles from the mission to the waiting Yankee ships that carried them to New England shoe manufacturers.

"This was the way they were got down — thrown down one at a time, a distance of 400 feet," wrote Dana. "Down this height we pitched the hides, throwing them as far out into the air as we could; and as they were all large, stiff, and doubled like the cover of a book, the wind took them, and they swayed and eddied about, plunging and rising in the air, like a kite when it had broken its string."

San Gabriel Arcangel (fourth mission, 1771).

Location: 537 West Mission Drive in San Gabriel

Jedediah Smith, the first overland Yankee observer of the California missions, led his pack train of trappers down from the Sierras to Mission San Gabriel in 1826. The padres received hospitably this harbinger of the overland migration that would inundate California from the east in the 1850s.

The magnificent church that stands today at San Gabriel closely approximates what Jedediah Smith saw. A long Moorish-style structure, built with stone at its base and with bricks higher up, with slender capped buttresses, the church boasts six bells on a side campanario. One bell, which weighs a ton, can toll an Angelus that is clearly heard in the Pueblo section of Los Angeles, eight miles away.

MEMORIAL TO INDIANS
CALIFORNIA'S FIRST
CEMETERY
MISSION SAN DIEGO

(Preceding Page:) The beautiful bell wall of Mission San Diego has a sumptuous setting in the mission garden on the north side of the church. Lovely flowers bloom here the year around in the benign Southern California climate.

(Above:) This close-up view of Mission San Diego illustrates one aspect of the lovely natural setting of this mission, this view looking toward the basilica and bell wall.

(Below:) The basilica of Mission San Diego reflects the simple dignity of the mission churches. The San Diego mission was California's first church.

(Above:) The interior of the restored Padres' bedroom shows the simplicity that governed the lives of the early missionaries at San Diego.

(Below:) A general view of Mission San Diego de Alcala, showing the campanario, or bell wall, and the basilica entrance. The Padres' bedroom is at the right.

(Following Page:) San Luis Rey, the "king of the missions," is still impressive today. The church, seen here with its pleasing bell tower, is a blend of Spanish, Moorish, and Mexican architecture. The fountain in the foreground is all that remains of a once-extensive irrigation system.

(Above:) This is the padres' bedroom at San Luis Rey, primitive by today's standards. The bed is crisscrossed leather thongs. Other articles seen here are a brazier, at the foot of the bed for hot coals; a washstand, and a few pottery vessels. A small chest on the other side of the room completes the furniture.

(Below:) Historic photograph of friars in procession, once a common sight at Mission San Luis Rey.

(Above:) A young Franciscan brother stands beside the first pepper tree planted in California, inside the quadrangle of Mission San Luis Rey.

(Below:) The large and beautiful church at Mission San Luis Rey is shown in this photo, looking very much as it did when Indian converts worshipped there.

(Opposite:) The beautiful, weathered arches of San Juan Capistrano look out over the lovely gardens of the mission.

(Left:) Statue of Fr. Junipero Serra and Indian boy, on grounds of mission San Juan Capistrano.

(Below:) After an earthquake destroyed the magnificent church at Capistrano in 1812, divine services were returned to the little adobe church now known as "Father Serra's Chapel."

(Following Page:) The once-great church at Mission San Juan Capistrano now lies in stately ruins. Fabled as the home of the swallows, Capistrano gives off an aura of romance that touches visitors to the mission.

(Above:) Mission San Gabriel Arcangel as it appeared in 1832 in this oldest-known painting of any California mission. The scene is by Ferdinand Deppe, a German employed in Mexico.

(Below:) Mission San Gabriel Arcangel is older than the city of Los Angeles. The side door of its church, shown on the left in this picture, opened directly on El Camino Real, "The Kings Highway" that connected all the California missions.

(Opposite:) A feature of the old mission church of San Gabriel is the altar, with its six priceless statues in the reredos, as the vertical partition back of the altar is called.

In Memory of
ANTONIO
First Indian buried
in this Cemetery
Oct. 20, 1778
R.I.P.

(Opposite:) The graveyard at San Gabriel reflects a sad episode in the mission era. Thousands of Indians, primarily epidemic victims, were buried here.

(Right:) A gleaming, white marble statue of Father Serra, one of the mission pioneers, stands in the garden at San Gabriel Arcangel.

(Below:) The Indian cemetery at San Gabriel is now a lovely garden.

(Above, Left:) This picture shows the cactus and succulent garden at Mission San Gabriel.

(Below, Left:) This ancient Spanish cannon originally belonged to the soldiers guarding Mission San Gabriel.

(Right:) Junipero Serra, zealous pioneer of the California mission system, is honored more than once in statuary depicting his protective arm around an Indian boy. This bronze of Father Serra is in Brand Park, across the street from the grounds of Mission San Fernando.

(Below:) The so-called "long building", which faces the street at Mission San Fernando, contains the padres' living quarters, the winery and smoke room, and the hospice, where travelers were always welcomed without charge.

The church, now in the attentive care of the Claretian Fathers, was the creation of Father Antonio Cruzado, who completed the impressive structure in 1806. The striking narrow windows and fortress-like demeanor, unusual among the missions, are Cruzado's New World approximations of the Moorish cathedral at Cordova, the diocese where he had studied for the priesthood. The 1812 quakes topped the belltower, but the church remained standing.

For today's traveler the San Gabriel Mission is the most informative mission site in the Los Angeles region. The orange baptistry with its hammered copper font; the museum with its parchment, old books, and Indian paintings of the 14 Stations of the Cross; and the adjacent kitchen winery, gardens, and graveyard all suggest the scope of San Gabriel on the eve of secularization.

The mission was then producing some 50,000 gallons a year of the best wine then available in California. Grapes were grown from vine clippings first brought to California by Serra in 1769.

Unrivaled in total prosperity, San Gabriel included soap, tanning, and tallow works among its enterprises, and produced more grain between 1777-1832 than any other mission. Well ahead of the other missions in the growing of wheat, San Gabriel ranked second in production of other crops — barley, corn, beans, peas, lentils, and garbanzos. 2,333 fruit trees were planted for oranges, lemons, apples, pears, peaches, and figs.

The saddest testimonial at San Gabriel is a graveyard for 6,000 Indians, primarily epidemic victims. In California in 1769 there were an estimated 100,000 Indians, the most populous concentration of Indians in the United States, which had an estimated 900,000 Indians when the White man first settled on the eastern and western shores. In California during the mission era the white man's diseases, such as measles and smallpox, devastated whole Indian communities. The Indians had no natural immunities to these newly introduced microbes. When the question arises, "How did the Indian fare under the mission system?", the first answer must be: in any prolonged contact with white Europeans, regardless of nationality or colonial policy, the California Indian was doomed to near extinction by disease alone.

San Fernando Rey de Espana *(17th mission, 1797).*

Location: 15151 San Fernando Mission Boulevard, San Fernando.

To the Franciscan padre of the 18th century each day in the yearly calendar presented the dramatic appearance of a saint or angel to be recalled, a virtue of the Virgin to be remembered, or an event in Christ's life to be meditated upon. Life was defined by the drama of these reappearing subjects.

So it is not surprising that the padres reached primarily for the names of saints when founding missions. They invoked the saint as a protector for the venture. Though the True Cross *(Santa Cruz)*; qualities of the Virgin: The Immaculate Conception *(La Purisima Concepcion)* and Our Lady of Solitude *(Nuestra Senora de Soledad)*; and angels *(San Gabriel Arcangel, San Miguel Arcangel)* were honored, the majority of the 21 names went to saints, such as Saint Ferdinand, King of Spain. Ferdinand III of Castile was a 13th-century Spanish king noted for his successful wars against the Moors and for founding Spain's great University of Salamanca.

Both Serra and his successor Lasuen realized that eventually an inland chain of missions would be necessary to connect San Gabriel with the missions located around San Francisco Bay. Serra had gone to his reward by 1797 when the energetic Lasuen dedicated in one year four inland missions, of which San Fernando was the southernmost link.

The famous hospitality of the missions can be appreciated by today's traveler when he visits the two-story, 243-foot-long hospice that is the central building at San Fernando. So large was this structure, the largest adobe building in California, that it overshadowed the church even at the height of the mission's prosperity. After secularization, when roof tiles of the church were wantonly removed, causing rains to melt the adobe, the subsequent owners of the property, a land and water company and a ranch, found the hospice a valuable piece of real estate and consequently kept it intact and well maintained.

Today the hospice houses demonstration rooms that recall the mission activities, such as cattle hide processing, for which San Fernando was famous. Mission products found a ready market in the nearby pueblo of Los Angeles. By 1818 the mission had accumulated 21,000 head of livestock. Rawhide was crucial for some uses that an observer of today might not consider. For example, iron spikes were in short supply in that time and place, so strands of rawhide were frequently used in all types of construction to hold the members together.

Persons who know their California history and who may have thought that the first discovery of gold in California was at Coloma, in 1848, will be surprised to learn that gold was actually first found in 1843 on an outer rancho of the San Fernando mission. A ranch foreman gathering onions to season his food found himself dusting flakes from the vegetables. A mini-rush produced some gold that was assayed and shipped to the United States mint in Philadelphia, but the scale of the discovery was insufficient to excite the imagination the way James Marshall's nuggets did later.

In a quiet section of the garden at San Fernando rests a statue of founder Fermin Lasuen. Along with Serra, he is one of the giants of early California history. Born in Victoria, Spain, in 1736, Lasuen joined the Franciscan Order at an early age and volunteered for the American missions. He served for seven years in the Sierra Gordo missions in the Queretero State of Mexico, then another six years in Baja, California. When he became father president of the California missions after Serra's death, Lasuen founded nine new missions between 1786-1798.

Aside from founding new missions, he greatly expanded and enhanced the missions that Serra had started but only developed to a rough state. Lasuen advanced the livestock and grain agriculture and imported artisans from Mexico to teach the neophytes many valuable trades. But perhaps most important to the mission observer of today, Lasuen created the architecture that is the surviving remnant of the era.

San Buenaventura *(ninth mission, 1782).*

Location: On Main Street in Ventura, off U.S. Highway 101.

The name of Father Junipero Serra rightly survives as the most widely known person of the mission period. His story is best told in connection with the founding of his ninth and last mission, San Buenaventura, in 1782.

Serra was born on the island of Mallorca and entered the Franciscan order at Palma. Eventually he became a doctor of philosophy at the Lullian University with a high reputation for preaching. Imbued with a spirit of adventure, he hoped to serve in the New World or possibly even the China missions. He was sent to the College of San Fernando in Mexico City and to an eight-year stint in the primitive Sierra Gordo of the Queretero State. When the Franciscan Order was given charge of the Jesuit missions of Baja, after the Jesuits were expelled through manipulations in the Spanish court, Serra became Father President of the Baja missions, with headquarters at Loreto.

When the Spanish king decided to support the California mission venture, Serra and other planners in Loreto determined that the first three missions should be at San Diego, at the Bay of Monterey, (which, unknown to them, Sebastian Vizcaino had fancifully overrated as a port when he passed there in 1602), and at a midway point. They decided in advance that the midway mission would be named after St. Bonaventure.

(Following Page:) This is the beautiful fountain and a part of the lovely garden inside the quadrangle of Mission San Fernando.

The vicissitudes of actual mission founding in California caused St. Bonaventure to be the ninth, not the third. Serra and the governor were not in agreement over the merits of founding a mission in the populous Santa Barbara channel with so small a contingent of military.

The reader of mission history must appreciate that Serra's passion for founding missions and thereby saving souls knew no bounds. At the inauguration of Mission San Antonio de Padua, Serra hung a bell from an oak tree and, even before the pack train of mules had been unburdened, rang the bell wildly. His comrades protested that the mission had as yet neither church nor parishoners, but Serra replied, "Let me give vent to my heart which desires that this bell might be heard all over the world."

The site of Mission Buenaventura was a fertile plain within hearing of the ocean surf in one of the most populated Indian regions of California. The resident Chumash Indians were among the most advanced of the California tribes. They were known as skilled boat builders, constructing large canoes of pine planks and pitch, in which three or four men commonly rowed into the channel to fish. Many observers praised the speed and agility of these crafts. The Chumash also knew how to weave reed baskets that were watertight. They lived in igloo-style houses with doors, holes for windows, and reed mattresses for beds.

The mission ranked seventh in agricultural production, noted especially for its gardens with such exotics as tropical fruits, including banana, coconut, and sugar cane. Today the church looks much as it did during the mission era, with an unusual triangular design — said to represent the Trinity — on the front, and, to support the facade, thick buttresses, a legacy of the devastating earthquakes of 1812.

Santa Barbara *(tenth mission, 1786).*

Location: 2201 Laguna Street, Santa Barbara.

Since its completion in 1820, the church that padre Antonio Ripoll built for his Santa Barbara Mission has provoked wonder in travelers. How in frontier California was a church with a Roman temple facade and such stately lines constructed. Ripoll's source of inspiration was an 18th-century Spanish translation of *The Six Books of Architecture* by Vitrivius Polion written in 27 B.C. The work was accomplished by highly trained Chumash Indian craftsmen.

Today Santa Barbara, the only mission church with two towers, looks much as it did in 1820, though careful restoration with modern materials lessens the danger that earthquakes will again severely damage it, something that happened as recently as 1925. Before this church was completed in 1820, three earlier churches on the site were all knocked down by quakes.

Beyond the church itself, Santa Barbara was and is noted for its elaborate water system, the most complete of any mission. Parts of it are still in use. A system of dams, reservoirs, and aqueducts brought water from nearby Pendregosa Creek. One aqueduct led water to an ornate fountain in front of the church and then to the laundry, gardens, and fruit orchards. A second aqueduct carried drinking water to a settling tank and filtration system.

Santa Barbara was always an active and prosperous mission, partly because of its situation near a lively port. The attractive site, benign climate, ample water supply, and unusually intelligent and friendly Indians helped. The grounds never suffered the destruction that occurred at other missions after secularization because the property remained continuously in the hands of the Church, changing quietly from an Indian mission to a parish church for white settlers. Today the buildings house an impressive museum as well as the archives of the Franciscan order.

For the Indians of the Santa Barbara Mission, however, secularization in the 1830s was as disastrous as it was in all the mission communities. Before the white man came, the California Indian enjoyed a life of relative peace, often hungry but never starving, seasonally gathering berries, seeds, bulbs, game, fish, and fowl. The great forests of oak trees provided an acorn staple in the Indian diet. California tribes were neither fond of nor skilled in war.

The Spanish colonial intentions with respect to the Indians placed a high value on the health and welfare of these natives because Spain did not herself have the manpower to settle new territories. By contrast, the Americans pushing westward on the Great Plains had little need for the Sioux.

Why was the Indian attracted to the missions? He was drawn by gifts, the earnest manner of the padres, the intoxication of music and ritual, and the certainty of three substantial meals a day. When the Indian became a "neophyte", agreeing to receive his baptism, there was no returning to his earlier life. Anyone who strayed was hunted down by the soldiers and returned to the mission compound.

In the mission the Indian was required to work long, disciplined hours, quite unlike his former life of intense hunting and gathering activity followed by long periods of indolence. To some extent the Indian was a slave of the missions, at a time when slavery was widespread throughout the world, although the mission lands were in theory the property of the Indian, held in trust for him by the padres until such time as the Indian was capable of self-government. Then all the accumulated worldly goods would be turned over to him.

That day never came, as any reader of California history knows. The problem was partly in the temperament of the Indian, whose view of life was so alien to the strict disciplinary requirements of elaborate communal living. The California Indian in his earlier state had learned to live in harmony with his environment, but he was essentially a primitive, stone-age being entirely lacking in the sophistication and advanced arts and sciences that the Spanish had found in the Mayam and Aztec cultures of Mexico.

If the liberal governor Jose Figueroa had lived to implement secularization, the breakup of the missions might have proceeded in an orderly manner, as he intended, with property held secure by Indians. But after his untimely death the factions vying for power complicated the secularization process and all pretense of orderly procedure disappeared. Some Indians with skills learned at the missions were able to make the transition, but for most the dilemma was tragic: the orderly but austere life they had known at the missions had come to an end, but in a generation of dependence on the mission they had lost the self-reliant, self-sufficient attributes that had enabled them to survive for thousands of years. And the environment for that kind of primitive survival was also disappearing rapidly. For most mission Indians freedom was a prelude to their own destruction.

Santa Ines *(19th mission, 1804).*

Location: 1760 Mission Drive, Solvang, 3 miles east of Buellton.

Santa Ines is the third and last mission whose name honors a woman. A 13-year-old martyr executed in Rome in 304 A.D., St. Agnes was the daughter of a noble Roman family. She refused to sacrifice to the pagan gods and died for her faith.

The setting was hospitable but off the main traveled routes, resulting in a somewhat lonely prosperity. An assignment to Santa Ines was not for the gregarious padre who favored the company of other educated Europeans. Arrival of a visitor at Santa Ines was an occasion rather than a mundane event. An Indian stationed in the bell tower would ring the bells, with a different code for a padre, a white man, and an Indian. Everyone turned out to greet the newcomer.

Churches built through 1812 were promptly shaken down by earthquakes, but the present structure, started in 1813 and completed in 1817, survived. The bucolic setting of the mission makes it a favorite for many present-day travelers. A museum contains a notable collection of vestments, church records, and missals.

(Left:) What remains of one of the unique wooden bells of San Buenaventura hangs as a very tired reminder of times long past, as seen in the mission museum.

(Below:) Mission San Buenaventura, located in the city of Ventura, looks much as it did during the mission era.

(Opposite, Above:) The restored padres' kitchen at Mission Santa Barbara may be seen in the old cloister wing, now an excellent museum.

(Opposite, Below:) The cloister garden of Mission Santa Barbara is especially beautiful. It is situated in the enclosed quadrangle back of the old church and cloister wing.

A campanario with three bells rises above a small graveyard. The unassuming facade of the church has an honesty that charms, with some echoes of Mission San Gabriel apparent. Inside, the church greets the visitor as it did an Indian in the 1800s, its straightforwardness softened with a concession to frivolity by its French crystal chandeliers.

The visitor of today who measures with his eye the L formed by the church, sacristy, and arcade of rooms off the church can get a good sense of the original size of the quadrangle by considering the L as one quarter of the original. Additional adobe barracks outside the courtyard housed 450 Indian neophytes.

Built at a favorable time when established missions lent ample materials and Indian laborers, Santa Ines prospered rapidly and eventually became fourth in agricultural production. 13,000 livestock roamed the mission lands. Artisans were brought from Mexico to teach the Indians. In a typical contract a carpenter was brought to California with the understanding that he would teach his trade to 12 Indians in four years.

Santa Ines is one mission in which a Yankee played a role. Joseph Chapman was serving an apprenticeship with the feared pirate Hippolyte Bouchard, who was pillaging the California coast at the time, but seeing that employment along those lines was uncertain, he jumped ship during a Bouchard raid and went straight. Santa Ines employed him as a handyman and vine planter. Eventually he married a daughter in the respected Ortega family.

The Indians at Santa Ines revolted in 1824, provoking a battle here and at La Purisima. Tensions underlying the rebellion were creating havoc throughout the mission system. After New Spain (Mexico) declared its independence from Spain in 1821, Spain withheld any further payments to the missions and to the soldiers stationed in California. The task of supporting the soldiers then fell on the missions, which meant that the burden rested squarely on the back of the Indians. To the Indians, who received little but abuse from the soldiers, the idea of now supporting the soldiers was intolerable. Because the soldiers were under the command of the governor and not the padres, the padres could not control or discipline the soldiers when incidents with the Indians occurred. Over one of these innumerable incidents, a mission guard flogging a neophyte corporal, the revolt began.

Another political factor that operated to destroy the mission system was Spain's practice of giving posts of civil authority in New Spain (Mexico) and in California only to the Spanish-born, who, presumably, would be more dependably loyal. The Franciscan padres had also been born in Europe. Consequently, an entire class of Mexico-or-California-born men, called creoles, barred from prominent civil posts, looked with enmity upon the Europe-born civil servants and padres. Though not rigorously enforced, one of the early Mexican laws after the break from Spain called for the expulsion of all Europe-born people in California.

La Purisima Concepcion (11th mission, 1787).

Location: Four miles northeast of Lompoc, 19 miles west of Buellton via State Highway 246.

If a traveler who wants to get the best possible sense of the California missions could visit only one site, there is no question but that La Purisima Concepcion should be the choice. Today, the mission is a 966-acre State Historic Park, completely reconstructed and restored during the 1930s by the Civilian Conservation Corps.

Today at La Purisima you can see how hides were processed to form the "California banknotes" that were the currency of the mission when bartering with Yankee trading ships. A re-created tallow works shows how the animal fat was rendered to make material for soap and candles. Candle works, weavery for wool blankets and cotton clothing, complete gardens of plants used by the missions, and an olive crusher are but a few of the attractions. The rustic setting of La Purisima can mesmerize the observer into believing that the Indian neophytes are out working in the fields and will return soon, pulling a load of produce in a carreta, their wood-wheeled cart. A fiesta in May recreates the mission crafts and practices.

La Purisima has several unique features, primarily the design of dedicated padre Mariano Payeras, who shepherded the mission from 1803 until his death in 1823. Founded in 1789, then refounded four miles away in 1815, La Purisima enjoyed a rapid prosperity, with livestock herds reaching 20,000 by 1810. Ten acres of vines produced wine grapes. But the dominant natural catastrophe of the mission period, earthquake, struck ferociously on December 21, 1812, as already noted in other mission sketches. At La Purisima, as if quaking alone was insufficient havoc, the quake opened up, in the hills, a natural dam impounding waters swollen by rains. Water cascaded over the ruins.

The padres were faced with a grim situation: they had 1,000 Indians to feed, clothe, and house, but their entire physical plant was destroyed. For the rebuilding they chose the new site four miles away.

The new mission departs in a striking manner from the square, cloistered patterns of other missions. To make escape routes in case of earthquake more accessible, they laid out the entire mission in straight lines and heavily buttressed the walls. Instead of arches and arcades, they favored a square beam method of roof support.

Prosperity quickly returned to La Purisima, but the interlude of plenty was to be brief. The padres restored an elaborate irrigation system including a drinking water filtration apparatus that percolated the water through three feet of sand and charcoal. The church has no pews, as was the custom, with Indians kneeling or sitting on the floor, men on one side, women and children on the other. Grain and fruit production soared in this fertile "Valley of the Watercress", as the region was known.

But gradually a litany of disasters encroached on the well-being of La Purisima. A drought in 1816-17 decimated the flocks. Fire in 1818 destroyed some of the buildings. Spurred by their grievances against the soldiers (not the padres), the Indians rebelled in 1824 and held La Purisima for a month as their fortified stronghold until the superior firepower of presidio soldiers sent from Monterey overcame them. For the Indians who lingered around La Purisima after secularization, a smallpox epidemic in 1844 completed the destruction.

San Luis Obispo de Tolosa *(fifth mission, 1772).*

Location: In San Luis Obispo, corner of Monterey and Chorro streets.

The California state animal, the grizzly bear, ironically now extinct within the borders of the state, played a crucial role in the early history of Mission San Luis Obispo.

When Governor Gaspar Portola made his first arduous trip to search for Monterey Bay in 1769, pushing himself and his men to the limit of their supplies, he passed through this region and found tule bulbs everywhere uprooted and the ground pocked with large footprints. Eventually he came upon the cause of this activity, a troop of grizzly bears, feeding on succulent roots. Portola's men naively thought in this first encounter that the silvertips could be dropped like deer with their muskets. When the first bear was wounded, he charged the startled party, killing one of the horses before a volley of shots brought him down. Portola named the region the Valley of the Bears, *La Canada de Los Osos.*

(Following Page:) Beautiful Mission Santa Barbara—"the Queen of the Missions"—is seen past spacious lawns and the Father Serra Memorial Cross.

Later, after the founding of Mission San Antonio de Padua, when that mission suffered a drought that brought its personnel to near-starvation, the Valley of the Bears was recalled, and a hunting party set out. The hunters returned with 4½ tons of dried bear meat, plus 25 bushels of edible seeds that were gained by trading bear meat with the Indians, who appreciated having the Spaniards challenge their mortal enemies.

The goodwill of the Indians was assured by this incident of the hunt when Fr. Serra founded the mission (his fifth), in 1772. He named it after St. Louis, Bishop of Toulouse, born in 1274.

The mission was the first to introduce on an elaborate scale what is considered a fixture of mission life, the red clay roof tile. This innovation, first used on the modest adobe chapel at Mission San Antonio de Padua, was employed at San Luis as a response to necessity. The original roofs of the missions were made of tules stretched across wood beams, but this roofing had two limitations: first, the rain could permeate the tules and begin to melt the adobe walls, and second, as the padres of San Luis learned on a night in November 1776, the flaming arrows of unfriendly Indians could easily set the tules on fire and burn the mission down.

Understandably, some Indians felt ambivalent about their comrades who joined the mission. To embrace the mission was to forsake an ancient way of life. Add to this the expected feuding between neighboring tribes, even though the California Indians were not warlike, and you have the minor rivalries and hatreds that led some enemies of the neophytes of San Luis to put a torch to the mission.

The padres, recalling that clay tiles graced their familiar structures in Europe, reasoned: why not make such clay tiles here? Soon the plans were put into effect, with horses' hooves marching endless circles, mixing the water and clay earth. Indians fashioned the clay over 22-inch wood molds that tapered from 12 to 20 inches. After the tiles were fired, they were ready for use. The practice of using clay tiles quickly spread throughout the mission chain.

San Luis is an interesting illustration of just what happened to the missions after secularization. On the eve of that transition, 1835, the grounds and holdings were valued at 70,000 uninflated dollars. But after the Indians were told the property was theirs for the taking and various hostile bands spirited away the livestock, the physical plant and resources dwindled rapidly. When the mission was put up for public sale in 1845 it was bought for only $510.

The mission then suffered the usual decline until it became the center of a flourishing small town, with the French Hotel located opposite it in 1875. In the 1870s and 80s the decaying church suffered the ravishing of a modernizer, which was, in some respects, more unkind than mere benign neglect. This modernizer covered the facade with white clapboard and erected a New England-style church steeple on the belltower. He redid the roof beams and interior ceiling in tongue-in-groove wood, painted the altar and reredos white, and generally transformed the mission to an appearance distinctly un-Californian.

San Miguel Arcangel *(16th mission, 1797).*

Location: Off U.S. Highway 101, 8 miles north of Paso Robles.

In the busy summer of 1797, as Fr. Fermin Lasuen sought to close the gaps on the inland mission route from north to south along the El Camino Real, he founded, as his third effort, Mission San Miguel Arcangel, completing the northern mission chain from San Luis Obispo to Dolores in San Francisco. From this mission there were ambitious plans to extend inland eventually to the Tulares region, approaching present-day Fresno, but the Indians were not always agreeable and the mission system was destined to collapse before such undertakings could be realized.

Prosperity gradually came to San Miguel. Its Indians were cooperative, with 15 baptisms the first day and 1,000 converts in four years. Other missions contributed supplies. The area was naturally blessed with good soil and adequate water. A raging fire of 1806, which destroyed hides, grain, and wool, was one dramatic setback in an ascending record of productivity that ranked San Miguel ninth in agriculture and livestock. The extensive ranches of the mission stretched for 50 miles north to south.

The church and part of the arcades still remain. The arcades are odd because each arch is a different size, but the church is noteworthy as the best available example today of misson art. Because the church, built 1816-1818, remained unattended for long periods in the 19th century, and allowing for its location on the north-south road, it is remarkable that no vandals destroyed the highly ornate work of the church interior, completed by Indians under the direction of a professional artist, Estevan Munras.

To gaze today at the 144-foot-long interior, the walls and ceiling excellently preserved, is to leap momentarily back to the California of the 1830s. The ceiling consists of 28 rafter beams with rough scrolls at the end. Each beam was cut from a single sugar pine trunk logged in the Santa Lucia Mountains, 40 miles west. The walls are covered with false perspective and trompe l'oreil pillars, balconies, and designs of leaves and tassels. The colors are bright red from various rocks, blues from wildflowers, plus some greens and pinks. The reredos, the framed structure back of the altar, boasts a dazzling mix of colors, imitation marble pillars, and intricate geometric designs. Rays of light from a hypnotic all-seeing eye of God over the statue of St. Michael must have bewitched the neophytes. Colors were applied with a glue made from cattle bones or were painted fresco-style on damp plaster.

That secularization was not always viewed as desirable from the point of view of the Indians it was meant to assist can be seen in an incident at San Miguel in 1831. The first governor sent from Mexico after the territory of New Spain became the country of Mexico was Jose Echeandia. When he issued a decree in 1831 allowing freedom for all Indians who desired it, a commissioner came to San Miguel with the announcement. After the Indians did not respond affirmatively, the commissioner dramatically requested that all those who favored the present system stand to the left, those who wanted their freedom move right. Not an Indian moved right.

San Antonio de Padua *(third mission, 1771).*

Location: Six miles west of Jolon in Monterey County.

When Serra was frustrated by the governor in his wish to found a third mission midway between San Diego and Carmel, he directed his energies instead toward starting a mission south of Carmel in a region of grassland and oak trees amidst rolling hills. He named this third mission San Antonio de Padua in 1771.

San Antonio de Padua was dedicated to a saint known as "the miracle worker" and the dedication itself appeared to be a fortunate one for the mission, when Serra sighted an Indian during the first mass. However, the actual conversion rate proceeded slowly with 18 neophytes in 2½ years. In 1782 the roof was covered with the first tiles used in mission

(Following Page:) The unassuming facade of Mission Santa Ines has a charming honesty, with few concessions to the more frivolous architectural touches.

(Following Page, Above Right:) At one time the antique, weathered look of the colonnade of arches at Santa Ines, as shown in this historic photograph, was fascinating to artists and photographers. After restoration was completed they are no longer in imminent danger of falling down, but not half as picturesque.

(Following, Below:) The three-bell campanario of Santa Ines has a straightforwardness in keeping with the other mission structures.

(Opposite:) Mission La Purisima Concepcion did not survive the ravages of earthquakes, fires, and time. The buildings were restored during the 1930s.

(Above:) This is one of the rooms in the old cloister at San Luis Obispo. The heavy walls made of stone, brick, and mortar are typical, with the whole plastered over.

(Below:) At Mission San Luis Obispo were made the first red roof tiles, now a familiar fixture of mission architecture.

(Following Page:) A stately colonnade of arches embellishes the Moorish-style Mission San Miguel Arcangel.

(Above:) The interior of the mission church at San Miguel has the only unretouched wall and ceiling decorations to be found in any of the California missions.

(Below:) Much of Mission San Miguel is original. Here is the present visitors' entrance, and, in the background, the colonnade of arches and the side of the old church.

(Opposite:) The cemetery at San Miguel is along the north side wall of the church, the preferred site of the mission padres. By 1833, the cemetery held the bodies of 2,249 Indians.

(Preceding Pages:) Mission San Antonio de Padua has been completely restored, with little that is different from the active mission days.

(Left:) Soledad Mission is in the process of being rebuilt. One of the few artifacts remaining from the original mission is the bell shown in this picture.

(Below:) Soledad, one of the loneliest of the missions — as its name implies — was built in 1791 and partly restored in 1955. Here we see the rebuilt chapel and the long porch of the restored cloister wing.

(Opposite:) The Carmel Mission, on a splendid site at the mouth of the Carmel Valley, has recaptured its former stateliness through careful restoration. Note the star window over the arched doorway with its huge, hand-carved doors.

(Following Two Pages:) Carmel Mission served as the headquarters of Father Serra, the father president of the mission system. The padre lies buried at this mission, the one he loved best.

architecture. Eventually, aided by a complex water system that dammed the San Antonio River, the mission prospered until it counted 17,491 livestock and 1,300 Indians. A water-powered grist mill ground the mission's wheat.

One of the most lengthy records of service in the missions occurred at San Antonio, where one of the priests who joined Serra at the founding, Buenaventura Sitjar, stayed for 37 years. The stability and continuity of Sitjar's administration allowed him to develop many amenities, such as a 400-page grammar and vocabulary of the native Mutsun Indian language, which aided in the translation of spiritual and temporal teachings.

The church was known for its campanario, or bell holder, located directly in front, the bells hanging in the wall over the arches.

So rapid was the disintegration of San Antonio after secularization that in 1845 when the mission was offered for sale, there were no takers. The ranchers who took over the mission area forced the Indians to revert to their native state, a transition few were prepared for. Because the mission was so isolated, its buildings and properties were quickly plundered of all materials of any value.

A competent and successful restoration effort started in 1907 and received strong funding in 1948. Today the church and quadrangle of the mission are lovingly restored. with a museum displaying several intriguing artifacts. A thoroughly bucolic setting gives the mission great appeal. The visitor should be forwarned that more than one photographer in the region, arriving near sunset because he was detained over back-country roads, has trained his camera in the appealing final minutes of bright light on what he believed was the mission, but which was in fact a Spanish-style officer's club for the nearby military establishment. Tank tracks and buzzing helicopters occasionally jar the colonial aura of San Antonio.

The area is a favorite for northern California residents with an appreciation for spring wildflowers. After a wet winter the grasslands near San Antonio abound not only with the common poppy and lupines, but also with such relatively rare flowers as Golden Blazing Star, *mentzelia lindleyi*.

Nuestra Senora de la Soledad *(13th mission, 1791).*

Location: On Ft. Romie Road, three miles northwest of Soledad.

The name given to this 13th of the missions is both fitting and accidental. When the great Franciscan diarist, Juan Crespi, passed through here in 1769 he understood that the natives called themselves by a name similar to the Spanish word for solitude, *soledad*. Two years later, when Junipero Serra was questioning an Indian woman in the area about her name he got the impression that she, too, had used a word like *soledad*.

Consequently, one of the attributes of the Virgin, Our Lady of Solitude, was bestowed on the mission at its founding by Fr. Lasuen in 1791. And a fitting name it was, then and now. So lonely and unpleasant was life at Soledad that mission fathers assigned there repeatedly requested transfers. A total of 30 padres served Soledad in the 44 years of its existence.

(Preceding Two Pages:) The very long cloister wing of Mission San Juan Bautista is seen across the only remaining Spanish plaza in California.

(Preceding Single Page, Left:) The reredos above the altar in the church of San Juan Bautista was built and decorated by Thomas Doak in 1820, the first United States citizen to settle in California.

(Preceding Single Page, Right:) Mission Santa Cruz as it stands today is only a partial, half-scale replica of the original, which disappeared completely after numerous indignities suffered by earthquake, tidal wave, and a plundering populace.

They complained often of rheumatism, and the traveler visiting Soledad today can understand why. The site can be excessively damp, whipped by unceasing winds, or else bone dry. Crops of alfalfa and wine grapes come nearly to the mission's edge. The absence of inviting human artifacts or natural features makes the traveler want to get back in his car and drive on. Many 19th-century observers of Soledad characterized it as the most lonesome, forlorn place they had seen in California.

But the lands were fertile, then as now, and Soledad achieved a middling prosperity vis-a-vis the other missions. About 20 acres of vineyards were planted, but the idea of growing grapes in the valley in the 20th century didn't catch on until the 1960s. Today the Salinas Valley around the mission grows 35,000 acres of prime varietal table grapes, which will favorably affect the wine palate of Americans in the coming decade, especially for fruity white wines. The padres built an irrigation system that flumed water from five miles away. Soledad accumulated 6,200 sheep by 1832, a time, surprising to say, that the market price for a sheep was twice the price of a horse.

A series of misfortunes plagued the Soledad Mission, starting in 1802 with a dread epidemic, the most feared unknown for mission Indians. In an age before vaccination, prayers were thought to be the only effective remedy. Floods came next, in 1824 and 1828, ruining the crops and badly damaging the buildings. The church collapsed in 1831, but a storehouse was quickly converted into a chapel. After secularization and the usual decline, Soledad was sold in 1846 for a mere $800.

Today Soledad has the chapel and one wing of the quadrangle completely restored, and houses a small but growing museum. The old church, at the opposite end of the restored cloister wing from the chapel, still has its tile floor, covered with a protective layer of sand. Extensive landscaping, well maintained, has changed the lonely spot to an oasis.

But the wind still blows. The traveler, carefully holding his hat, may ponder the eternal verities while gazing at the mounds of melting adobe on the other three sides of the quadrangle. The motto of the nearby town of Soledad says it all, "May the wind be always at your back."

San Carlos Borromeo de Carmelo *(second mission, 1770).*

Location: 3080 Rio Rd., Carmel.

The Carmel Mission, as this longer-named mission is often called, satisfies as few other missions can, largely because of its appealing mix of history, architecture, and setting.

A mission on Monterey Bay was the second to be founded by Fr. Serra, in 1770, to satisfy the rationale of the mission system from the Spanish king's point of view. Monterey Bay was the northernmost-known suitable site to occupy if Spain wanted to forestall further encroaching advances of the Russians and possibly ambitious English to the north.

After an initial mission site near the Monterey Presidio proved unwise (the Indians reacted with alarm to the noise of the soldiers' guns and the soldiers' conduct had a bad influence on the neophytes), Serra moved the mission to an attractive valley along the Carmel River, five miles away.

From his headquarters here at a rude thatch and wood church, Serra managed the growing mission chain, which numbered nine units by the time he died here, at age 71, after 15 years of service in California. Serra had overseen the baptism of 5,307 Indians. Only 5 feet, 2 inches in height, Serra was blessed with a rugged constitution and proved

(Following Page:) Mission Santa Clara is on the campus of the University of Santa Clara. Today's university chapel, built after a fire in 1926, is a faithful reproduction of the old mission church. The bell tower contains the original bells sent from Spain.

to be an indefatigable walker around California, though hampered by a lame leg that plagued him from his early days in Mexico and was apparently due to infection after an insect bite.

The otherworldly scope of Serra's ambition can be assayed by gazing at his spartan lodging at Carmel, which consists of little more than a plank bed and writing table. To his successor, Fr. Fermin Lasuen, went the task and honor of transforming the rude church on the site to the stone monument where Serra is buried and where so many admirers of the mission pass a pleasant hour. The mission's progress was hampered somewhat by a damp climate, which slowed agricultural production, and by the small number of Indians who lived in the area.

After secularization the Carmel Mission decayed quickly, with bean fields planted right up to the front door of the church. In 1882 a steeply pitched roof was added, protecting the stone buildings from further weather damage, but as a "restoration" the style was inappropriate. Finally, in 1934, a competent restoration began.

The 1797 church shows the skilled hand of Manuel Ruiz, a professional stone mason brought from Mexico in 1791. The exterior tower is Moorish in character and the front is adorned with a star window. An elegant fountain, olive trees, and attractive gardens enhance the site. One chapel in the church displays a statue of the Virgin that Serra brought to San Diego and subsequently Carmel.

While most of the other mission restorations show today only the church or chapel and a wing of quadrangle, the beautiful Carmel Mission presents the complete quadrangle courtyard typical of mission architecture. The guiding hand here, as with most other California mission restorations, was that of Harry Downey, still sexton at Carmel as this is written.

Set on rising cypress-covered hills, "two gunshots" from the sea, the Carmel Mission has a simple picturesqueness that is satisfying but stops short of becoming cloying. The mission comes alive on the last Sunday in September at the annual fiesta honoring St. Charles Borromeo.

San Juan Bautista *(15th mission, 1797).*

Location: On the town square in San Juan Bautista, off State Highway 156.

No California mission has a stronger feeling of continuity than San Juan Bautista, in use as a parish church since its founding by Fermin Lasuen as the 15th mission, in 1797. Beyond its continuing pastoral role, the church has also served primarily a Mexican-American congregation. To witness the fiesta here at the Virgin of Guadalupe, December 12, honoring this patroness of all Mexico and the Indians, transports a modern observer back 180 years.

In addition to the mission, part of the adjacent town of San Juan Bautista, laid out around the plaza, has been preserved (as a state historic park). The restoration includes a hotel, stable, and two adobe houses.

Because the church is located directly on the granddaddy fault, the San Andreas, one might expect that its history would be focused around piles of debris, however, a preliminary quake in 1800 warned the padres that their later designs for a massive three-aisled church were too ambitious. Wiser than they knew, for their ostensible reason was the decline in the neophyte population, they walled in the supporting arches which separated the outer aisles from the nave. When the great tremblor of 1906 leveled much of northern California, this center section survived, although the outer walls of both side aisles collapsed.

A Yankee, California's first United States settler, made a small contribution to San Juan. Thomas Doak, after jumping ship at Monterey in 1818, was in such penurious straits that he agreed to paint for board-and-room the altar reredos of San Juan in bright blue and red colors that can be seen today. His offer underbid a Mexican laborer, who required 75 cents per day. It will be interesting in some future century for participants in a ceremony at San Juan to unearth from the cornerstone a bottle, sealed in the adobe in 1803, describing the event.

San Juan Bautista blossomed with a modest prosperity. The mission was noted especially for its cooperative Indians, but disliked for its ravenous fleas, which attacked many 19th-century travelers without discrimination according to race, color, or creed.

Throughout the mission system the one aspect of civilized life that reached a high form of expression was music. Father Estevan Tapis, himself a trained musician, fostered the musical arts at San Juan. The California Indian took to music more readily than to any other aspect of European culture. Many of the missions had elaborate choirs of Indians and some, such as San Jose, had extensive holdings in instruments, such as violins, violas, trumpets, and flutes. Tapis introduced an ingenious colored notation system that allowed his Indians to read music easily. Today some of his patiently lettered parchments still survive, with the different voice parts in red, white, black, and yellow. The tradition that Tapis began had such longevity that 40 years after secularization there were still Indians singing in the San Juan Bautista parish choir.

An incident at San Juan illustrated the proverb that music soothes the savage breast. A band of Tulare Indians on the warpath arrived at the mission with violence in their hearts, but when the padre went out to meet them with a barrel organ, secured in trade from a whaling or exploring ship, the Indians found their aggression transformed hypnotically to a delight in the musical airs. They threw down their arms, sang loudly, and bloodshed was averted. The barrel organ may still be seen at the mission today.

Like many missions, San Juan suffered from the well-intentioned assault of a "modernizer", this time in the person of one Father Rubio. In 1865 Rubio determined that the mission bells, hanging by leather thongs from a crossbar, should be elevated above the church in a more dignified New England-style steeple. In various later versions, some more "mission-like", the steeple persisted. Finally, in 1949 the bells were moved down from the belfry to their original crossbar. For the bells of San Juan it was crossbar to crossbar in three generations.

During 1976 and 1977 the earthquake damage done in 1906 to the side aisles of the mission church was at last repaired. Adobe bricks which had supported the arches so well, but separated the three aisles, were knocked away. Once again San Juan Bautista is the largest California mission church, the only one with three aisles. Once again the bells left their crossbar, but this time were lifted to a new bell wall compatible in design with Spanish times.

Santa Cruz (12th mission, 1791).

Location: Emmet and High streets, Santa Cruz.

After an auspicious beginning, Santa Cruz suffered just about every indignity that could befall a mission. When Fermin Lasuen established this 12th mission in 1791, the initial work of conversion and building progressed rapidly. Grass, game, berries, and redwood or pine lumber were readily available. Vegetables grew well in the fertile soil. But progress gradually tapered off, and Santa Cruz had only 430 neophytes at its most populous moment.

The first blow came in 1797 when the governor, skipping over a law that required a pueblo to be a league from a mission, established the town of Branciforte closely adjacent to Santa Cruz. The situation at best would have been trying, had the residents of Branciforte (a name honoring the king's viceroy in Mexico), been upstanding. But the populace sent to what was supposed to be a model city proved, in fact, to be indolent vagabonds.

The expected friction between neophytes and Brancifortians reached a high point in 1818 when the pirate Hippolyte Bouchard was sighted off the coast. The governor, pre-

(Opposite:) The garden and bell tower of Mission Santa Clara present a peaceful scene against the blue California sky.

(Right:) The old monastery at Mission San Jose now houses an interesting museum.

(Below:) Not much remains of Mission San Jose de Guadaloupe — in fact, only a small part of the quadrangle wing where the padres' living quarters were. Plans are being made to rebuild the mission church.

suming that Bouchard would land and plunder Santa Cruz, ordered the padre to retreat with his charges to Santa Clara, which he did, leaving the Brancifortians in charge.

Only too late did the padre realize this tactical error. He returned to find that Bouchard had not landed, but that the Brancifortians themselves had laid waste to the mission, drinking all the wine and brandy, scattering valuable relics, and plundering whatever could be carried away. The padres pleaded with the governor either to move the pueblo or allow the mission to be abandoned, but the governor refused both requests, leaving the Franciscans impaled on the horns of their dilemma.

In 1825 quakes weakened the buildings. After the repairs were completed, a tidal wave came up the river and undermined the structures, causing the bell tower to collapse in 1840. A quake leveled what still remained standing in 1857. Not only were roof tiles and lumber spirited away, but even the stones of the foundations.

In 1931 a half-size replica of the original church was completed near the original site, The little cloister wing contains a small museum.

Santa Clara de Asis *(eighth mission, 1777)*.

Location: In Santa Clara on the campus of the University of Santa Clara.

By the Franciscans' own measure of success, the number of heathens baptized into Christianity, Santa Clara exceeded every other mission. Between the founding in 1777 and the end in 1832, 8,536 Indians were baptized there. Santa Clara also ranked fourth in total livestock among the missions in 1832.

Originally both missions San Jose and Santa Clara were authorized by the viceroy in Mexico as perimeter fortifications for the Yerba Buena and Mission Dolores communities located near the tip of the San Francisco peninsula.

Santa Clara prospered, because of the cooperation of the Indians, fertility of the land, and able leadership of the padres. The mission artisans were known for their weavings.

The church that stands today is a 1929 replica of the original 1825 church, which was itself the fifth church for the Santa Clara Mission. The first rough church was on the Guadalupe River. Flood, quake, fire, and inappropriate site choices forced the mission to move frequently in the first decades.

A gifted painter from Mexico, Agustin Davila, was brought in to teach the Indians painting and to oversee painting the facade and interior roof of the 1825 church. The 1925 replica repeats his facade designs, but in three-dimensional concrete rather than in paint. The interior still boasts a reredos done as a duplication, an early crucifix, and a duplication of the Davila ceiling designs.

After secularization, the church and grounds were eventually given to the Jesuits, who founded a college which later became the University of Santa Clara.

San Jose residents benefited in the 19th century from an arborial creation of the mission fathers and their charges, who planted a string of willows along the miles between the pueblo of San Jose and the mission. This grand promenade is now a prominent street, the Alameda. The padres hoped that such a clearly marked road would aid the wavering faithful in pueblo San Jose in finding their way to Sunday mass, especially in the heat of the summer sun.

Mission Santa Clara counted an unusual number of characters and eccentrics among its padres. First, there was Magin de Catala, who became known as The Prophet. It is said that he predicted correctly the arrival of Americans, discovery of gold, loss of California by Spain, and destruction of San Francisco by the earthquake and fire of 1906. Then there was Jose Viader, a priest who might have followed another calling as a wrestler. In 1814 he was attacked by an Indian brute, named Marcelo, and his two companions. The muscular Viader promptly thrashed the three of them, forgave them for their assault, and thereafter counted Marcelo as one of the mission's faithful supporters.

San Jose de Guadalupe *(14th mission, 1797).*

Location: In Fremont, at Highway 238 and Washington Boulevard.

The Biblical maxim that the first shall be the last surely applies to Mission San Jose de Guadalupe. To the visitor of today the remains of this mission appear meager — only a small part of the quadrangle wing, which now houses a museum with a pounded baptismal font; altar bells, vestments from the mission era, and some Mexican statuary. In back of this adobe can be seen a tangle of olive trees, remnants of better days.

But Mission San Jose in 1832, on the eve of secularization, had reached a level of achievements that few missions could match. It ranked third behind Santa Clara and San Gabriel in converts: 6,673. It was third also in livestock holdings, 24,180 head in 1832. In total agricultural production it was second only to San Gabriel by 1832.

When San Jose de Guadalupe was founded in 1797 the mission and adjacent pueblo were envisioned as a base from which the troublesome tribes of the inland valleys could either be converted or subdued. A mission here would reduce the costs involved in arming pack trains. In the first year there were only 35 converts at the mission, but that number increased rapidly. Military expeditions were continually being sent to punish harassing tribes from the inland areas, but the Indians, skilled at blending into the grassland maze of the Delta could easily escape their pursuers.

For 27 years San Jose de Guadalupe received its guidance from one of the Renaissance men of the Franciscan order, Fr. Narciso Duran, who directed the elaborate mission enterprises, planned military campaigns against hostile Indians, constructed irrigation systems, and wrote and taught music. The inventory at the time of secularization indicates what remained of Duran's elaborate Indian orchestra, which had drawn so many favorable comments. In 1832 the mission had 20 violins, 4 bass viols, 1 contra bass, 1 drum, 1 hand organ, 1 book of choral music, and 26 band uniforms. Duran also served two terms as father president of the missions.

After secularization, the mission church became a parish church, the orchards and fields were tended by squatters for a few additional years, and an arcade of the mission became a Mexican hotel. Slow disintegration received a dramatic acceleration in 1868 when California experienced its greatest quake in recorded history, a massive tremblor along the Hayward Fault, of larger magnitude even than the 1906 quake that destroyed San Francisco. This great quake toppled the mission church. A wooden structure, now abandoned, was later built in its place. It is scheduled to be moved as elaborate plans take shape to rebuild the old mission church on its original foundations.

San Francisco de Asis *(sixth mission, 1776).*

Location: 16th and Dolores Street, San Francisco.

The discovery of the great San Francisco Bay, the "port of ports", large enough to "hold all the ships of Spain," came rather late in California colonial history. Spanish explorer Sebastian Vizcaino in 1602 so overrated Monterey Bay that when the first overland traveler, Gaspar Portola, arrived there, he didn't recognize it. English explorer-pirate Sir Francis Drake sailed his *Golden Hind* into what is now Drake's Bay at Point Reyes in 1579 to make repairs, but he apparently didn't discover San Francisco Bay.

(Following Page Above:) The interior of the old Mission Dolores church shows extensive use of redwood in the construction. The church is the oldest building in San Francisco.

(Following Page Below:) Mission Dolores, in San Francisco, is little altered from the time it was completed in 1791, despite the passing of time and the quake and fire of 1906.

(Following Right-hand Page:) Mission San Raphael Arcangel is another mission that disappeared completely. The chapel seen here is on the approximate site, more a memorial to the mission than an actual reconstruction.

When Portola finally did discover San Francisco Bay on his second trek north and determined that it was indeed a bay, the Spanish viceroy in Mexico quickly took advantage of the strategic importance of the area and directed that two missions and settlements be founded there without delay.

So in 1776, the climax year of revolutionary fervor on the eastern shore of North America, Juan Bautista de Anza led 240 settlers on one of the most remarkable overland treks in western history. Starting from the Sonora state of northwest Mexico, De Anza carefully guided his charges and about 1,000 livestock to Monterey. Considering the distance and the sometimes hostile terrain, it is remarkable that the De Anza expedition reached its destination with more settlers than they set out with, their numbers augmented by births along the way. The expedition eventually left Monterey and founded the town by which San Francisco was first known, Yerba Buena, or the good herb, a plant suitable for medicinal tea. Mission San Francisco de Asis, the presidio, and the pueblo were all formed in 1776.

The first mission church was a 50-foot-long log and mud affair and was moved eventually because the lowland swamp site was not suitable. The adjacent stream and small lake named Dolores soon furnished a second name to the mission. The church that one sees today was started in 1782 and completed 1791. While the quadrangle has long since disappeared and the surrounding buildings have also changed with the passing of time and the quake of 1906, the mission church has remained little altered, its exterior a statement of honest simplicity with Corinthian pillars and its interior a repository of Indian-designed chevrons painted on plain ceiling beams. The reredos behind the altar and paintings on the wall are fine examples of early California art.

The Mission's activities were crippled by attrition and by disaster. Though the mission reached a peak number of 1,800 neophytes in 1823 and in total recorded 6,898 baptisms in its long history, success was diminished by the poor agricultural conditions caused by chilly fogs. A measles epidemic in 1804 and again in 1826 contributed to the total of 5,500 Indian burials there. Defection of neophytes was frequent because of the attractive and relatively carefree life that an Indian could enjoy around lush San Francisco Bay. The number of neophytes at San Francisco de Asis at the time of secularization was a mere 204.

Chill fogs and persistent sea winds had a continuing adverse effect on the health of the Indians attracted to Mission Dolores. This situation caused the padres to look for a sunny new mission site to the north where sick Indians could recuperate.

San Rafael Arcangel (20th mission, 1817).

Location: Fifth Avenue and Court Street, San Rafael.

Both the padres and the civil authorities agreed that a hillside on the eastern shores of the peninsula north of San Francisco had the qualities of the climate that sick Indians at Mission Dolores needed: warmth, sun, and dryness.

So acute and chronic was the problem of illness among the Dolores Indians that the governor readily agreed to the founding of a branch mission, named after the Archangel Raphael, whose name means "healing power of God".

While the Franciscans considered benevolent care of the Indians a sufficient reason for establishing the new asistencia, the civil authorities, who sometimes viewed the native with suspicion at best and contempt at worst, required further motivation. The needed incentive came from their fears that the expansion-minded Russians, who had established an outpost north of San Francisco at Fort Ross in 1812, conducting their fur trade in otter skins and also planting grain, would extend further into Spanish territory. Spain wanted to establish a firmer claim to the land, by right of occupation, and new missions north of San Francisco would be the most economical means.

The physical plant at San Rafael was never imposing; just a small church, with star windows modeled after Carmel, a bell hung on wood cross beams, and one long wing with priest quarters, shops, a chapel, and the infirmary. The healthful climate and the skills of the one padre in California who had medical training, Luis Gil y Taboado, succeeded in curing the Indians. Other missions began sending their sick, and by 1823 San Rafael was officially raised in status from merely an outlying infirmary to a mission in itself. Eventually San Rafael became self-sufficient, noted for its pears, and reached a maximum population of 1,140, primarily Coast Miwok Indians, by 1823.

The first mission to be secularized, San Rafael's livestock, property, even the vines and fruit trees, as well as the Indians fell into the hands of General Mariano Vallejo in Sonoma. He put the Indians to work on his vast ranches. In 1846, when the American period in California history was about to open, Captain John Fremont stayed briefly in the declining buildings at San Rafael, biding his time. By 1870 the structure was torn down so that the wood could be salvaged.

The chapel at the approximate site today duplicates some of the characteristics of the original mission church, such as the star windows and the bell hung from cross beams.

San Francisco Solano *(21st mission, 1823).*

Location: In Sonoma, off the Plaza.

In 1823, fear of Russian expansion reached such a level in the mind of Governor Don Luis Arguello that he listened to an ambitious young Franciscan, Jose Altimira, propose that Dolores and San Rafael be closed and a new mission founded farther north. Altimira, last of the Spanish Franciscans, had been stationed at Dolores and found the setting disagreeable.

Acting without the knowledge or approval of Father President Senan, Altimira began the mission. As Senan lay dying he learned of the scheme and rebuked both the governor and Altimira. After negotiations between all parties, it was agreed that neither Dolores nor San Rafael would be suppressed, but that San Francisco Solano would be allowed. The Russians surprised everyone by donating a bell and utensils.

Building progressed rapidly, and within a year a wooden church, granary, and priest's quarters were completed. However, Altimira showed little tact in dealing with the Indians, resorting often to flogging and imprisonment, until in 1826 the Indians rose up and literally forced him to flee to San Rafael. Eventually he returned to Spain. Despite efforts to revitalize the mission, the pressures of secularization soon overwhelmed it.

The church currently seen at the site is an 1840s parish church for Sonoma, adjacent to an adobe section of the mission quadrangle. Today the mission is a state historic park with an informative, small museum. After secularization, the monastery served as a blacksmithy and the priest quarters became a site for wine making and hay storage.

The administrator for the secularized mission was General Mariano Vallejo, who removed to his ranches the Indians, cattle, and fruit trees of the mission. Vallejo was a *Californio*, as the Spanish in California were called, who was destined to play a strong role in the transition of California from Mexican to United States rule. Near the mission site in 1846 a group of American partisans who had captured Vallejo raised a crude flag with a picture of a bear on it, though some would argue that the animal's features were unintentionally porcine. So occurred the famous Bear Flag Revolt and its inauguration of a California Republic. Before the *Californios* could muster their forces to do battle with the Bear Flaggers, the landing of the United States marines at Monterey put an end to this brief vision of California as a separate country.

(Following Page:) Mission San Francisco Solano de Sonoma.